9

D1481721

WITHDRAWN

50 POEMS

Osip Mandelstam

50 POEMS

Translated by Bernard Meares
Introductory Essay by Joseph Brodsky

PERSEA BOOKS
NEW YORK

For information, address the publisher:
  Persea Books, Inc.
  Box 804 Madison Square Station,
  New York, N.Y. 10010

International Standard Book Number: 0-89255-006-6, paper
                                    0-89255-005-8, cloth
Library of Congress Catalog Card Number: 76-52274

FIRST EDITION

Printed in the United States of America

Contents

Introduction

For some odd reason, the expression "death of a poet" always sounds somewhat more concrete than "life of a poet." Perhaps this is because both "life" and "poet," as words, are almost synonymous in their positive vagueness. Whereas "death"—even as a word—is about as definite as a poet's own production, i.e., a poem, the main feature of which is its last line. Whatever a work of art consists of, it runs to the finale which makes for its form and denies resurrection. After the last line of a poem nothing follows except literary criticism. So when we read a poet, we participate in his or his works' death. In the case of Mandelstam, we participate in both.

One should bear that in mind while turning these pages, which are so light. Even if it is true that "he became his admirers," their total number is far less interesting than his concise version of them. I am saying this not out of humility (which admirers, especially when totalled, are always lacking), nor because there is no substitute for a genius (and there really is none). I am saying this because what matters in art is precisely the unique, unrepeatable, unresurrectible mixture of flesh and spirit, and what makes the achievements of the latter all the more precious is the very moribundity of the former.

A work of art is always meant to outlast its maker. Paraphrasing the philosopher, one could say that writing poetry, too, is an exercise in dying. But apart from pure linguistic necessity, what makes one write is not so much a concern for one's perishable flesh but the urge to spare certain things of one's world—of one's personal civilization—from one's own nongrammatical continuum. Art is not a better, but an alternative existence; it is not an attempt to escape reality but the opposite, an attempt to animate it. It is a spirit seeking flesh but finding words. In the case of Mandelstam, the words happened to be those of the Russian language.

For a spirit, perhaps there is no better accommodation: Russian is a very inflected language. What this means is that the noun could easily be found sitting at the very end of the sentence, and that the ending of this noun (or adjective or verb) varies according to gender, number, and case. All this provides any given verbalization with the stereoscopic quality of the perception itself, and (sometimes) concretizes and develops the latter. The best illustration of this is Mandelstam's handling of one of the main themes of his poetry, the theme of Time.

There is nothing odder than to apply an analytic device to a synthetic phenomenon; for instance, to write in English about a Russian poet. But it wouldn't be much easier to apply such a device in Russian either. Poetry is the supreme result of the entire language, and to analyze it is but to diffuse the focus. It is all the more true of Mandelstam, who is an extremely lonely figure in the context of Russian poetry, and it is precisely the density of his focus that accounts for his isolation. Literary criticism is sensible only when the critic operates on the same plane of both psychological and linguistic regard. The way it looks now, Mandelstam is bound for a criticism coming only from below in either language.

The inferiority of analysis starts with the very notion of theme, be it a theme of time, love, or death. Poetry is, first of all, an art of references, allusions, linguistic and figurative parallels. There is an immense gulf between *homo sapiens* and *homo scribens* because for the writer the notion of theme appears as a result of combining the above techniques and devices, if it appears at all. Writing is literally an existential process; it uses thinking for its own ends, it consumes notions, themes, and the like, not vice versa. What dictates a poem is the language, and this is the voice of the language, which we know under the nicknames of Muse or Inspiration. It is better, then, to speak not about the theme of Time in Mandelstam's poetry, but about the presence of Time itself, both as the entity and the theme, if only because Time has its seat within a poem anyway, and it is a caesura.

So, because of that, Mandelstam, unlike Goethe, never exclaims "O moment, stay! Thou art fair!" but merely tries to extend his caesura. What is more, he does it not so much because of this moment's particular fairness or lack of fairness; his concern (and subsequently his technique) is quite different. It was the sense of an oversaturated existence that the young Mandelstam was trying to convey in his first two collections, and he chose the portrayal of overloaded Time for the medium. Using all the phonetic and allusory power of words themselves, Mandelstam's verse in that period expresses the slowing-down, lasting sensation of Time's passage. As he succeeds (which he always does), the effect is the reader's realization that the words, even their letters—vowels especially—are almost palpable vessels of Time.

On the other hand, his is not at all that search for bygone days with its obsessive gropings to recapture and to reconsider the past. Mandelstam seldom looks backward in a poem; he is all in the present, in this moment, which he makes continue, linger beyond its own natural limit. The past, whether personal or historical, has been taken care of by the words' own etymology. But however unProustian his treatment of Time is, the density of his verse is somewhat akin to the great Frenchman's prose. In a way, it is the same total warfare, the same frontal attack—but in this case, an attack on the present, and with resources of a different nature. It is extremely important to note, for instance, that in almost every case when Mandelstam happens to deal with this theme of Time, he resorts to a rather heavily caesuraed verse which echoes hexameter either in its beat or in its content. It is usually an iambic pentameter lapsing into alexandrine verse, and there is always a paraphrase or a direct reference to either of Homer's epics. As a rule, this kind of poem is set somewhere by the sea, in late summer, which directly or indirectly evokes the ancient Greek background. This is partly because of Russian poetry's traditional regard for the Crimea and the Black Sea as the only available approximation to the Greek world, of which these places—Taurida and Pontus Euxinus—used to be the outskirts. Take, for instance, poems like "The stream of the golden honey was pouring so slow . . . ," "Insomnia. Homer. Tautly swelling sails . . . ," and "There are orioles in woods and lasting length of vowels" where there are these lines:

> But once a year Nature is bathed in length,
> Which is the source of Homer's metric strength.
> Like a caesura that day yawns wide,

9

The importance of this Greek echo is manifold. It might seem to be a purely technical issue, but the point is that the alexandrine verse is the nearest kin to hexameter, if only in terms of using a caesura. Speaking of relatives, the mother of all Muses was Mnemosyne, the Muse of Memory, and a poem (be it a short one or an epic) must be memorized in order to survive. Hexameter was a remarkable mnemonic device, if only because of being so cumbersome and different from the colloquial speech of any audience, Homer's included. So by referring to this vehicle of memory within another one—i.e., within his alexandrine verse—Mandelstam, along with producing an almost physical sensation of Time's tunnel, creates the effect of a play within a play, of a caesura within a caesura, of a pause within a pause. Which is, after all, a form of Time, if not its meaning: if Time does not get stopped by that, it at least gets focused.

Not that Mandelstam does this consciously, deliberately. Or that this is his main purpose while writing a poem. He does it offhandedly, in subordinate clauses, by the act of writing (often about something else), *never* by writing to make this point. His is not topical poetry. Russian poetry on the whole is not very topical. Its basic technique is one of beating around the bush, approaching the theme from various angles. The clear-cut treatment of the subject matter, which is so characteristic of poetry in English, usually gets exercised within this or that line, and then a poet moves on to something else; it seldom makes for an entire poem. Topics and concepts, regardless of their importance, are but material, like words, and they are always there. Language has names for all of them, and the poet is the one who masters language.

Greece was always there, so was Rome, and so were the biblical Judea and Christianity. The cornerstones of our civilization, they are treated by Mandelstam's poetry in approximately the same way as Time itself would treat them: as unity—and *in* their unity. To pronounce Mandelstam as adept at either ideology (and especially at the latter) is not only to miniaturize him, but to distort his historical perspective, or rather his historical landscape. Thematically, Mandelstam's poetry repeats the development of our civilization: it flows north, but the parallel streams in this current mingle with each other from the very beginning. Toward the Twenties, the Roman themes gradually overtake the Greek and biblical references, largely because of the poet's growing identification with the archetypal situation of "a poet versus Empire." Still, what created this kind of attitude, apart from the purely political aspects of the situation in Russia at the time, was Mandelstam's own estimate of his work's proportion to the rest of contemporary literature, as well as to the moral climate and the intellectual concerns of the rest of the nation. It was the moral and the mental degradation of the latter which were suggesting this imperial scope. And yet it was only a thematic overtaking, never a takeover. Even in "Tristia," the most Roman poem, where the author merely quotes from the exiled Ovid, one can trace a certain Hesiodic patriarchal note, implying that the whole enterprise was being viewed through a somewhat Greek prism. Later, in the thirties during what is known as the Voronezh period, when all those themes—including Rome and Christianity—yielded to the "theme" of bare existential horror and a terrifying spiritual acceleration, the pattern of interplay, of interdependence between those realms, becomes even more obvious and dense.

It is not that Mandelstam was a "civilized" poet, he was rather a poet for and of civilization. Once, on being asked to define Acmeism—the literary movement to which he belonged—he answered: "nostalgia for a world culture." The notion of a world culture is distinctly Russian. Because of its location (neither East nor West) and its imperfect history, Russia has always suffered from a sense of cultural inferiority, at least toward the West. Out of this inferiority grew the ideal of a certain cultural unity "out there" and a subsequent intellectual voracity toward anything coming from that direction. This is, in a way, a Russian version of Hellenisticism, and Mandelstam's remark about Pushkin's "Hellenistic paleness" was not in vain.

The mediastinum of this Russian Hellenisticism was St. Petersburg. Perhaps the best emblem for Mandelstam's attitude toward this so-called "world culture" could be that strictly classical portico of the St. Petersburg Admiralty decorated with reliefs of trumpeting angels and topped with a golden spire with a silhouette of the clipper at its tip. In order to understand his poetry better, the English-speaking reader perhaps ought to realize that Mandelstam was a Jew who was living in the capital of Imperial Russia, whose dominant religion was Orthodoxy, whose political structure was inherently Byzantine, and whose alphabet had been devised by two Greek monks. Historically speaking, this organic blend was most strongly felt in Petersburg, which became Mandelstam's "familiar as tears" eschatalogical niche for the rest of his not-that-long life.

It was long enough, however, to immortalize this place, and if his poetry was sometimes called "Petersburgian," there is more than one reason to consider this definition both accurate and complementary. Accurate because, apart from being the administrative capital of the empire, Petersburg was also the spiritual center of it, and in the beginning of the century the streams of that current were merging there the way they do in Mandelstam's poems. Complementary because both the poet and the city profited in meaning by their confrontation. If the West was Athens, Petersburg in the teens of this century, was Alexandria. This "window on Europe," as Petersburg was called by Voltaire, this "most invented city," as it was defined later by Dostoevsky, lying at the latitude of Vancouver, in the mouth of a river as wide as the Hudson between Manhattan and New Jersey, was and is beautiful with that kind of beauty which happens to be caused by madness—or which tries to conceal this madness. Classicism never had so much room, and Italian architects who kept being invited by successive Russian monarchs understood this all too well. The giant, infinite, vertical rafts of white columns from the facades of the embankments' palaces belonging to the Czar, his family, the aristocracy, embassies, and the *nouveau riches* are carried by the reflecting river down to the Baltic. On the main avenue of the empire—Nevsky Prospect—there are churches of all creeds. The endless, wide streets are filled with cabriolets, newly introduced automobiles, idle, well-dressed crowds, first-class boutiques, confectioneries, etc. Immensely wide squares with mounted statues of previous rulers and triumphal columns taller than Nelson's. Lots of publishing houses, magazines, newspapers, political parties (more than in contemporary America), theaters, restaurants, gypsies. All this is surrounded by the brick Birnam woods of the factories' smoking chimneys and covered by the damp, gray, widespread blanket of the Northern Hemisphere's sky. One war is lost, another—a world war—is impending, and you are a little Jewish boy with a heart full of Russian iambic pentameters.

In this giant-scale embodiment of the perfect order, iambic beat is as natural as cobblestones. Petersburg is a cradle of Russian poetry and, what is more, of its prosody. The idea of a noble structure, regardless of the quality of the content (sometimes precisely *against* its quality, which creates a terrific sense of disparity—indicating not so much the author's but the verse's own evaluation of the described phenomenon), is utterly local. The whole thing started a century ago, and Mandelstam's usage of strict meters in his first book, *Stone,* is clearly reminiscent of Pushkin, and, that of his Pleiade. And yet, again, it is not a result of some conscious choice, nor it is a sign of Mandelstam's style being predetermined by the preceding or contemporary processes in Russian poetry.

The presence of an echo is the primal trait of any good acoustics, and Mandelstam merely made a great cupola for his predecessors. The most distinct voices belong to Derzhavin, Baratynsky and Batiushkov. To a great extent, he was acting very much on his own in spite of any existing idiom—especially the contemporary one. He simply had too much to say to worry about his stylistic uniqueness. But this overloaded quality of his otherwise regular verse was what made him unique.

Ostensibly, his poems did not look so different from the work of the Symbolists who were dominating the literary scene: he was using fairly regular rhymes, a standard stanzaic design, and the length of his poems was quite ordinary—from sixteen to twenty-four lines. But by using these humble means of transportation he was taking his reader much farther than any of those cozy-because-vague metaphysicists who called themselves Russian Symbolists. As a movement, Symbolism was surely the last great one (and not only in Russia); but poetry is an extremely individualistic art, it mocks isms. The poetic production of Symbolism was as quantitative and seraphical as the enrollment and postulates of this movement were. This soaring upward was so groundless that graduate students, military cadets, and clerks felt tempted, and by the turn of the century the genre was compromised to a degree of verbal inflation, somewhat like the situation with free verse in America today. Then, surely, devaluation as reaction came, bearing the names of Futurism, Constructivism, Imagism. Still, these were the isms fighting isms, devices fighting devices. To my taste, only two poets, Mandelstam and Tsvetaeva, came up with a qualitatively new content, and their fate reflected in its dreadful way the degree of their spiritual autonomy.

In poetry, as anywhere else, spiritual superiority is always disputed at the physical level. One cannot help thinking it was precisely the rift with the Symbolists (not entirely without anti-Semitic overtones) which contained the germs of Mandelstam's future. I am not referring so much to Georgi Ivanov's sneering at Mandelstam's poem in 1917 which was then echoed by the official ostracism of the thirties, but to Mandelstam's growing separation from any form of mass production, especially linguistic and psychological, the result was an effect in which the clearer a voice gets, the more dissonant it sounds. No choir likes it, and the aesthetic isolation acquires physical dimensions. When a man creates a world of his own, he becomes a foreign body against which all laws are aimed: gravity, compression, displacement, and annihilation.

Mandelstam's world was big enough to invite all of these. I don't think that had Russia chosen a different historical path, his fate would have been that much different. His world was too autonomous to merge. Besides, Russia went the way she did, and for Mandelstam, whose poetic development was rapid by itself, that direction could bring only one thing—a terrifying acceleration. This acceleration affected, first of all, the character of his verse. Its sublime, meditative, caesuraed flow changed into a swift, abrupt, pattering movement. His became a poetry of high velocity and exposed nerves, sometimes cryptic, with numerous leaps over the self-understood, with somewhat abbreviated syntax. And yet in this way it became more a song than ever before, not a literary but a birdlike song, with its sharp, unpredictable turns and pitches, something like a goldfinch tremolo.

And like that bird, he became a target for all kinds of stones generously thrown at him by his motherland. It is not that Mandelstam opposed the political changes taking place in Russia. His sense of measure and his irony were enough to acknowledge the epic quality of the whole undertaking. Besides, he was a paganistically bouyant person, and, on the other hand, whining intonations were completely usurped by the Symbolist movement. Also, since the beginning of the century, the air was full of loose talk about a redivision of the world, so that when the Revolution came, almost everyone took what had occurred for what was desired. Man-

delstam's was perhaps the only sober response to the events which
shook the world and made so many thoughtful heads dizzy:

> So we might as well try setting sail:
> Huge and clumsy creaks the turning wheel . . .
>
> (The Twilight of Freedom)

But the stones were already flying, and so was the bird. In the
translator's introduction, the reader of this book will find some
descriptions of their trajectories. Still, it is important to note that
Mandelstam's attitude toward a new historical situation: on the
whole he regarded it as just a harsher form of existential reality, as a
qualitatively new challenge. Ever since the Romantics we have had
this notion of a poet throwing down the glove to his tyrant. Now if
there ever was such a time at all, this sort of action is utter nonsense
today: tyrants are not that available any longer. The distance be-
tween us and our masters can be reduced only by the latter, which
seldom happens. A poet gets into trouble because of his linguistic,
and, by implication, his psychological superiority, rather than his
politics. A song is a form of linguistic disobedience, and its sound
casts a doubt on more than a concrete political system: it questions
the entire existential order. And the number of its adversaries
grows proportionally.

It would be a simplification to think that it was the poem against
Stalin which brought about Mandelstam's doom. This poem, for all
its destructive power, was just a by-product of Mandelstam's treat-
ment of the theme of this not-so-new era. For that matter, there is a
much more devastating line in the poem called "Ariosto" written
earlier the same year (1933): "Power is repulsive as were the
barber's hands . . ." There were others, too. And yet I think that by
themselves these mug-slapping comments wouldn't invite the law
of annihilation. The iron broom that was walking across Russia
could have missed him if he were merely a political poet or a lyrical
poet slipping into politics. After all, he got his warning (see the
translator's introduction) and he could have learned from that as
many others did. But he didn't, because his instinct for self-
preservation had long since yielded to his ethics. It was the im-
mense intensity of lyricism in Mandelstam's poetry which set him
apart from his contemporaries and made him an orphan of his

epoch, "homeless on an all-union scale." For lyricism is the ethics of language, and the superiority of this lyricism to anything that could be achieved within a human interplay is what makes for a work of art and lets it survive. Because of that, the iron broom, whose purpose was the spiritual castration of the entire populace, couldn't have missed him.

It was a case of pure polarization. Song is, after all, restructured Time, toward which mute Space is inherently hostile. The first has been represented by Mandelstam, the second chose the State as its weapon. There is a certain terrifying logic in the location of that concentration camp where Osip Mandelstam died in 1938: near Vladivostok, in the very bowels of the state-owned Space. This is about as far as one can get from Petersburg inside Russia. And here is how high one can get in poetry in terms of lyricism (the poem is in memory of a woman, Olga Vaksel, who died in Sweden, and was written while Mandelstam was living in Voronezh where he was transferred from his previous place of exile near the Ural Mountains after having a nervous breakdown). Just four lines:

> . . . And stiff swallows of round eyebrows(*a*)
> flew(*b*) from the grave to me
> to tell me they've rested enough in their(*a*)
> cold Stockholm bed(*b*).

Imagine a four-foot amphibrach with altered (*a b a b*) rhyme.

This strophe is an apotheosis of restructuring Time. For one thing, language is itself a product of past. The return of these stiff swallows implies both the recurrent character of their presence, and/or the simile itself, either as an intimate thought or a spoken phrase. Also, "flew . . . to me" suggests spring, returning seasons. "To tell me they've rested enough" too suggests past, past imperfect because not attended. And then the last line makes a full circle because the adjective "Stockholm" exposes the hidden allusion to Hans Christian Andersen's children's story about the wounded swallow wintering in the mole's hole, then recovering and flying home. Every schoolboy in Russia knows this story. The conscious process of remembering turns out to be strongly rooted in the subconscious memory and creates a sensation of sorrow so piercing, as if this is not a suffering man we hear, but the very voice of his wounded psyche. This kind of voice surely clashes with everything, even with its medium's—i.e., poet's—life. It is like Odysseus tying himself to a mast against the call of his soul; this—and not only the fact that Mandelstam is marrried—is why he is so elliptical here.

He worked in Russian poetry for thirty years, and what he did will last as long as the Russian language exists. It will certainly outlast the present and any subsequent regime in that country, both because of its lyricism and its profundity. Quite frankly, I don't know anything in the poetry of the world comparable to the revelatory quality of these four lines from his "Verses on the Unknown Soldier," written just a year prior to his death:

> An Arabian mess and a muddle,
> The light of speeds honed into a beam—
> And with its slanted soles,
> A ray balances on my retina . . .

There is almost no grammar here but it is not a modernistic device, it is a result of an incredible psychic acceleration, which at other times was responsible for the breakthroughs of Job and Jeremiah. This honing of speeds is as much a self-portrait as an incredible insight into astrophysics. What he heard at his back "hurrying near" wasn't any "winged chariot" but his "wolf-hound century," and he ran till there was Space. When Space ended, he hit Time.

Joseph Brodsky
New York, 1977

Translator's Introduction

OSIP MANDELSTAM, born in Warsaw on January 3, 1891, first made his mark on Russian literature in 1910 as one of the poets of the Acmeist group. (The other leading Acmeists were Anna Akhmatova and her first husband, Nikolai Gumilyov.)

Acmeism, with the stress it accorded to a down-to-earth representation of reality, had grown out of the symbolist school of Russian poetry, but while maintaining the symbolists' high literary standards, it rejected their self-indulgent mystical paraphernalia. Indeed, the connection between the two movements was so umbilical that some of Mandelstam's earliest poetry is symbolist in tone.

But Mandelstam quickly detached himself from the symbolists and developed his own theories about poetry, which fitted more easily into the loose garb of the Acmeists. At pains to point out the movement was not a poetic school, Mandelstam himself said of it much later: "Acmeism is for those who, filled with the spirit of building, do not cravenly reject the force of gravity pressing them down, but joyfully accept it, so as to awaken and utilize the architectural forces dormant within it."

In the nineteen-thirties, he went beyond even this, to weld his Acmeist theory into a criterion governing the fabric of civilization and history as a whole, declaring: "Acmeism is a nostalgic longing for world culture."

Given the fact the nineteen-thirties were the dead years, when Acmeism was a dirty word, when he and Anna Akhmatova, the two surviving unrepentant Acmeist poets of Russia, were subject to persecution, Mandelstam's statement was foolhardy. . . .

For those raised in the English-speaking world, it is difficult to comprehend that Russian poets have long had a political status as great as that of more public figures and that Russian poetry frequently has a political impact. Mandelstam actively avoided the political world, ran from the limelight, and felt uncomfortable in the presence of the powerful, but his verse stood in defiance of the currents of his times and the literary tastes fostered in his country.

Mandelstam recognized the importance attached to poetry in Russia: "only in our country is poetry respected," he once told his wife in the 1930s, "people are killed for it. And there's nowhere else that people are killed for poetry. . . ." Because he stood in such flat literary opposition to the cultural policies that gradually crept in after the early 1920s, Mandelstam was particularly singled out. In doing so, his literary-political foes conferred a political status on him, his every poem was bound to be seen as politically weighted, and eventually every line of his, published or unpublished, prose or verse, came to be regarded as subversive.

We must thus concede that in its effect, if not in its original intent, his poetry was political. If he had lived in the United States, Mandelstam would have been considered as an independent radical. He had been loosely associated with the Social Revolutionaries (SR's) during his youth. After the revolution he printed verse in a Left SR newspaper. He worked for six months in the People's Commissariat for Education. In the early 1920s he argued in support of the Soviet government, and believed in the Stalin constitution of 1936.

At the same time, even at its most politically respectable, his poetry remained ambivalent; it was often doomladen and despairing. The "Ode to Stalin," written to stave off his inevitable end in 1936, is ambivalent and sparked off a series of more genuine bitter poems that ran counter to its whole spirit. Part of the ode, which was believed to have been destroyed by his wife who considers it alien to the corpus of his work, was published in *The Slavic Review*, December, 1976.

Mandelstam, however, did not see himself as a political

poet. In the 1930s, he told Nikolai Khardzhiev, editor of the 1973 Soviet edition of his work, that he was the last Christian Hellenic poet in Russia.

His verse was first printed in 1909 when he was eighteen years old; by 1913 he had published his first collection, called *Kamen* (The Stone). This consists of symbolist verse, Acmeist poetic exercises in handling different techniques, and poetry echoing classical themes but written in a contemporary vein.

Though not switching masks as frequently as W.B. Yeats, for example, Mandelstam's poetic work underwent several major inner changes in the course of his life, notably as regards the denseness and type of imagery employed. Nevertheless, his general approach remained consistent. While experimenting with meter, he largely retained the accepted prosody of Russian. He introduced novel rhyme schemes and metrical patterns, but remained conventional enough in his structure, with certain major exceptions, such as "The Finder of a Horseshoe" (No. 24) and a few others in free verse; some in blank verse, like "Take for joy's sake, these hands of mine" (No. 16); and others which no more than hint at rhyme, such as "Stooping involuntarily to the empty ground" (No. 50).

Readers should be aware of the complex emotional and intellectual content of Mandelstam's verse, half-hidden in his thickets of imagery. They should remember that his verse is awash with concealed quotations, discreet or explicit, from Homer, Sappho, Pindar, Hesiod; from Ovid and Virgil; from Villon, Racine, Gautier, and Nerval; from Dante, Ariosto and Tasso; and from Derzhavin, Pushkin, Lermontov, Tyutchev, Blok, Akhmatova and Mayakovsky.

In the poetry Mandelstam wrote from 1916 onward, the gentle lightness present in *The Stone* gave way to foreboding, whether prophetic divination or from realization that Imperial Russia was breaking up under the burden of the Great War. The foreboding seeped into almost every verse he wrote, and by 1920 it was the leitmotif of his work.

Throughout his life he led a nomadic existence, the Civil War period being no exception. He wrote cycles of verse in Moscow in 1918, in the Crimea in the summer of 1920, and in Petrograd in the winter of 1920-21. These had coalesced into a single major group by the beginning of 1922, in which year most of his verse since 1916 was published as a collection called *Tristia*.

From 1921 onward his poetry underwent a sharp change. The imagery he used became less classical, more hieroglyphic; he felt himself out of joint with his times; he came to believe that the cultural values he held dear no longer had any validity. His work became harsher, his voice more plaintive; he was writing himself into silence. In "The Age" (No. 23) he spoke of his era as a beast with a broken back; in "The Finder of a Horseshoe" (No. 24), while he apologized for being out of step ("I myself went wrong, was mistaken, made an error in my calculations"), he described the world he knew as ending ("And the fragile chronography of our times is drawing to a close").

A poetic silence did ensue—from 1926 to 1930 he wrote no poetry. Nevertheless, Mandelstam actually published more during that period than ever before or ever again, most of it in 1928: second editions of both *The Stone* and *Tristia*, together with his verses from 1921-25, in a collection called *Poems*; a barely fictionalized account of his childhood in Saint Petersburg, called *The Noise of Time*, forming part of a slightly longer work, *The Egyptian Stamp*; and a book of critical essays, *About Poetry*.

One contributory factor to his poetic silence can be demonstrated. He was unmasked by extreme radical literary groupings as an "internal emigré," and persecution of him began to invade even his private life. A completely gratuitous charge of plagiarism involved him in energy-sapping petty litigation for over two years and merged with the campaign to consign him to literary oblivion.

By 1930, the campaign against him was reaching a crescendo, and he and his friends appealed for help to his one powerful protector, the Soviet leader Nikolai Bukharin, himself already a suspect figure. Bukharin was persuaded to send him off on a long trip to Soviet Armenia.

Mandelstam and his wife spent eight months under the glaring skies of that barren and ancient plateau. For Mandelstam the experience was a watershed.

In the first place, it resulted in *Journey to Armenia*, an

impressionistic prose sketch of Armenian life, whose publication in the journal *Zvezda* two years later was the last time for more than thirty years that work by Mandelstam appeared in print in the Soviet Union. Secondly, it resulted in his completing the strange work *Fourth Prose*, superficially an account of the charges of plagiarism leveled at him for his editing of a translation of Charles de Coster's *La légende de Thyl Ulenspiegel et de Lamme Goezak*, but more importantly a declaration of his position in relation to Soviet literature and to attempts to bury him. Thirdly, on the journey back from Armenia he began writing poetry again with a cycle called *Armenia*.

This was followed, apparently stimulated by the cathartic exercise of *Fourth Prose*, by poems with a pervading air of defiant confidence in his right to a place in the world, even as an outcast.

The poems he wrote during this period are clear, forthright, and bitter, and they culminated in the famous epigram on Stalin: *We live without feeling beneath us firm ground* . . . (No. 41) which, though heard by only eleven people, all except one of them close friends, resulted in Mandelstam's first imprisonment.

He was arrested on May 13, 1934, interrogated at the Lubyanka, but became the recipient of a minor act of clemency on the part of Stalin, who at a time when he was sending thousands to the labor camps, allowed himself to be pressured, probably by Bukharin and Pasternak, into exercising mercy. Mandelstam, who could have been given a severe sentence, was sent into banishment in the small town of Cherdyn' in the northern Urals.

Driven temporarily insane by the (comparatively lenient) treatment he had received in the Lubyanka, he tried to commit suicide shortly after arriving in Cherdyn', fearing a quiet execution "as soon as the publicity dies down," and unable to sleep for the hallucinatory voices of rumor that he was convinced he could hear on every side.

Stalin's act of clemency continued. As a result of further intercession on Mandelstam's behalf, perhaps by Bukharin, he and his wife were allowed to settle in Voronezh, a largish city on the border between Russia and the Ukraine.

Mandelstam's period of banishment there was to last until May 16, 1937, but he was now able to find occasional work and could be visited discreetly by his friends. Tardily, the Mandelstams began to build up a systematic archive, transcribing the poems Mandelstam still carried around in his memory, and resurrecting fragments of half-forgotten verses already noted down but confiscated after his arrest.

From the beginning of 1936 onward, Mandelstam was overtaken by his last great burst of poetic productivity. In terms of quantity alone, his output in the period was enormous. Between December, 1936 and May, 1937 he composed at least seventy of his more than 390 verses.

Despite the fact that 1937 was the height of the Great Purge, he was released from banishment in May, 1937 but as a former offender he was required to live more than 105 kilometres from Moscow.

There ensued a year of wandering from place to place around the forbidden 105 kilometre radius, with one lengthy spell of residence on the outskirts of Kalinin (Tver'). The Mandelstams lived on handouts, as nobody would employ him, even in a menial capacity, and as Nadezhda could not obtain work either. No poetry has survived from this period.

The age of clemency ended on May 2, 1938. Mandelstam was rearrested. Sentenced without trial to five years' hard labor for "counter-revolutionary activities," he was deported east towards Kolyma, the uttermost outpost of the prison empire.

He was apparently not fated to reach there. Though shadowy legends persisted about a lonely figure reciting verses to hardened criminals, and though a poet called Yury Dombrovsky is alleged to have collected Mandelstam's prison poems, slightly more reliable confirmation reached his wife that he was no longer in any condition to write poetry. The last communication from him was a desperate but lucid letter in the fall of 1938 stating that he was being held in a transit camp near Vladivostok for the winter, and that he urgently needed clothes, food, and money.

The probable date of his death was December 27, 1938, and the presumed place of his death was at the same transit camp, Second River, near Vladivostok, Soviet Far East.

Biographical Data

Date of birth:	January 3, 1891, Warsaw Father: leather merchant, self-educated in the German cultural mold, never fully Russianized Mother: completely within Russian cultural tradition, music teacher
1891-1907	Childhood in St. Petersburg, where he attends the Tenishev School (1899-1907), one of the most highly reputed schools in Russia.
1905	Witnesses the 1905 Russian Revolution
1907-10	Travel abroad: studies in Paris (winter 1907-8); Heidelberg (winter 1909-10), with brief visits to Switzerland and Italy (twice), and intermittent residence in St. Petersburg
1910	Poems first published in *Apollon*, St. Petersburg literary periodical
1911-16 (?)	Studies Greek erratically at University of St. Petersburg, never takes a degree
1911	Meets Akhmatova and Nikolai Gumilev, Acmeist poets
1913	Publishes *Stone*, first collection of verse First critical articles published

1914	Outbreak of First World War, works for St. Petersburg municipal war assistance services ("Union of Cities")
1915-16	Involved with Marina Tsvetayeva, poet
March 2, 1917	February Revolution. Abdication of Tsar
March-November	Provisional Government
November 7, 1917	October Revolution: Joins People's Commissariat for Education
May, 1918	Moves to Moscow, with the transfer of government ministries to the new capital
1918-22	Travels all over Russia during Civil War. Jailed by General Wrangel's Anti-Bolshevik White Guards in Crimea, and by authorities in Batumi.
Spring, 1919	Meets Nadezhda Khazin in Kiev; immediately begins lifelong marital relationship with her.
1923	Publishes *Tristia* (second collection) Writes *The Noise of Time*
1926-30 (Sept.)	Writes no poetry. Nomadic existence between the Leningrad area and Moscow.
1928	Mandelstam unfairly accused of plagiarism, castigated in the press
	Publishes: *Poems; About Poetry* (essays); *The Egyptian Stamp* (prose including *The Noise of Time*)
December, 1929	Begins dictating *Fourth Prose*
1930	Travels to Armenia for 8 months
Fall, 1930	Resumption of poetry
1932	Writes *Talk about Dante* (prose criticism)

Spring and summer, 1933	Holiday in Koktebel' and Stary Krym (Old Crimea), ancient capital of Crimea
	Publishes *Journey to Armenia* (last published work)
October, 1933	Composes "Epigram on Stalin" (No 286)
May 13, 1934	First arrest
June-September, 1934	Initial place of banishment: Cherdyn', Urals. Madness.
Fall, 1934	Transfer to Voronezh, southern Russia
1935-36	Reconstructs from memory confiscated verses, writes broadcast scripts Writes *First Voronezh Notebook* *Verses on the Unknown Soldier* Attempt to write *Ode to Stalin* *Second Voronezh Notebook*
May 16, 1937	Release from banishment
May, 1937-May 1938	Forced to live outside Moscow. No poetry has survived from this period.
May 2, 1938	Rearrest of Mandelstam, subsequently sentenced to five years' hard labor for "counter-revolutionary activities"
December 27, 1938	Official date of death. Presumed place of death, Transit Camp, Second River, near Vladivostok, Soviet Far East.

Translator's Note

N.B. The first of the two sets of numbers given in parenthesis follows the numeration utilized in *The Collected Works of Mandelstam*, Washington-New York Inter-Language Literary Associates, 1967-71. The second set of numbers, indicated with an asterisk (*), follows the numbering system employed in the 1973 Soviet edition of Mandelstam's poems. The numbers are given for reference; it must be recalled that there are slight descrepancies between the versions given in the two editions, and that neither edition is complete.

50 POEMS

HAGIA SOPHIA

I

Hagia Sophia: it was at this place
The Lord ordained that peoples and Caesars halt.
Your dome is, in a witness's phrase,
As if hung by a chain from heaven's vault.

And when Ephesian Diana allowed the looting
Of a hundred and seven green marble columns
For alien gods, it proved for ages yet to come
A monument to Justinian.

But what was it your generous builder meant
When he laid down apses and exhedrae,
As great his spirit as his intent,
Indicating to them east and west?

And bathing in the world, the shrine inspires awe,
Its forty windows are a celebration of light;
On the dome's supporting vaults, the four
Archangels cause the most delight.

And the wisdom of his hemispherical dome
Shall outlive peoples, outlast the ages still to come,
While the full-voiced sobbing of the Seraphim
Shall not let its darkened gilding dim.

(38, 34*)   1912

33

2

The idle life has sent us insane,
Wine in the morning, hung over by night,
How can pointless gaiety be restrained,
Your flushing face, plague-drunk again?

In handshakes at parting lies a torturing rite,
And in kisses in the street at night
When heavily the rivers flow
And streetlamps like ancient torches glow.

We lie in wait for death like a wolf of myth,
But I fear the one who'll first be dead
Is he whose lips are a care-racked red
And over whose eyes a long curl twists.

(44, 252*)   November, 1913

3

There are orioles in the forests and the only real measure
In tonic verse is the quantity of vowels.
But once a year Nature is bathed in length,
Which is the source of Homer's metric strength.

Like a caesura that day yawns wide,
From dawn there's repose and drowsy lengths of life;
The oxen are at pasture and at noon's golden tide
It would cost too much effort to draw a note from a fife.

(62, 55*)   1912 (?)

4

The bread is poisoned and the air's drunk dry,
How difficult to doctor wounds!
Joseph sold into Egypt
Could not have grieved so much for home!

Bedouin tribesmen with closed eyes
Compose wild legends as they ride
Beneath a star-studded sky,
About the troubled day gone by.

So little is needed for inspiration:
An arrow-quiver lost in the sands
Or a horse that someone has traded—
The fog of events is dispersing.

And if a song's properly sung
With a full heart, then at last
All disappears; there remain
Just the singer, space and the stars!

1913

Insomnia. Homer. Tautly swelling sails.
I've read the catalogue of ships half through:
This wedge of cranes, this outstretched brood
That once took wing across the Aegean isles.

A train of cranes outstretched towards alien frontiers,
The foam of gods crowns the leaders' kingly hair.
Where sail you to? If Helen were not there,
What would Troy mean for you, oh warriors of Greece?

Both Homer and the sea: all things are moved by love;
To whom shall I pay heed? Homer here is silent
And the dark sea thunders, eloquent,
And rumbling heavily, it breaks beneath my bed.

(78, 66*)   1915

6

In the polyphony of young girls' choirs
All tender churches sing in their own true voice,
And from the stone arches of the Assumption's tiers
I conjure up round brows and rejoice.

And from the vaults that archangels support
At some fantastic height I saw the city.
In the Acropolis walls I was by sadness gnawed
For a Russian name and for Russian beauty.

Is it not a wonder that we imagine gardens
Where pigeons flutter in the hot blue air
When the black nun sings from Orthodox notes?
Sweet Assumption—Florence in a Moscow square.

And Moscow's penticupolar cathedrals,
With their Italianate yet Russian soul,
Call forth for me a vision of Aurora,
But with a Russian name and in a coat of fur.

(84, 270*)   February, 1916, Moscow

7

In a sledge packed deep in straw we lurched
With the fateful matting scarcely covering us
All around enormous Moscow's arc
From the Sparrow Hills to a favorite church.

But in Uglich children play knucklebones,
There's an odor of bread left in stoves:
I'm borne through the streets bareheaded,
And three candles glimmer in a chapel.

It wasn't three candles burning but three meetings,
One of them blessed by God himself,
A fourth is not to be; Rome's far away,
And he never did love Rome anyway.

The sledge heaved into black ruts,
The people return from the fair,
And scraggy men and mean-looking shrews
Shifted from foot to foot at the gate.

The raw distance was dark with flocks of birds;
The thongs have cramped my knotted arms;
The prince is carried out; my body goes fearfully numb
As fire is set to the rust-red straw.

(85, 71*)   March, 1916

39

8 *SALOME*

I

When, sweet Salome, you can't sleep in your huge room
And wait, insomnolent, for the ceiling's fall,
With steady heaviness in that more saddening gloom,
Till it shall slowly downward on your fluttering eyelids fall,

Oh resonant Salome, like a hollow dried-out straw,
You've drunk the whole of death and become more tender still.
Snapped is that lovely lifeless straw,
Not Salomeia, no, but sweet Salome still.

In hours of sleeplessness all things acquire more mass,
As if there's less of them (so quiet it seems!).
The pillows gleam pallidly in your looking glass;
Reflected in its sluggish whirlpool, your bed can still be seen.

No, it isn't that Salome in solemn satin hung,
Above the black Nevá in that enormous room.
For twelve months long the hour of death's been sung
And pale blue ice streams into the gloom.

December in triumph is streaming out its breath
As if the heavy Nevá was flowing through the room.
No, not Salome nor a straw, but Ligeia—dying, death—
I've learned those blesséd words by heart.

II

I've learned those blesséd words by heart:
Eleonora, Salomeia, Ligeia, Seraphite;
The Nevá is flowing through that enormous room
And blue blood is streaming from the granite.

40

December triumphs above the Nevá's floes,
For twelve months long the hour of death's been sung.
No, it's not Salome in triumphal satin hung
Who tastes that lingering, wearying repose.

December Ligeia still lives within my brain;
Her blessèd love lies sleeping in a tomb,
But that sweet straw whose name may be Salome
Is killed by pity and shall not return again.

(86, 75-76*)   December, 1916

9

This night is beyond repair
But where you are light fills the air.
At Jerusalem's city gate
The black sun has risen in state.

More frightening is the yellow sun—
Sleep, my child, hush, little one—
In the light-filled Temple, Judaeans
Sang my mother's funeral paeans.

Deprived of redemptive grace,
No priests left to their race,
In the light-filled Temple they mourned
My mother and laid her to rest.

The voices of the Israelites
Over my mother's coffin rang;
I started awake in my cradle
Bathed by the black sun.

(91,-*)   1916

10

Among the priests and elders, the young Levite
Long into the morning watch remained,
While overhead thickened the Judaic night
And the broken Temple's veil rose sullenly again.

He said: The yellow heavens bode no good for us
And night has fallen on the Euphrates; oh priests, take flight!
The elders replied: The guilt is not in us;
For this, Judaea's joy, this black and yellow light,

Was also with us when, on the banks of the brook,
We swaddled the Sabaoth in fine muslin and took
The heavy seven-branched candlestick
To light the Holy City's night and the fumes of nonexistence.

(100, -*)   October or November, 1917

43

II

At a terrifying height, a wandering fire,
But does a star really glimmer that way?
Translucent star, O wandering fire,
Your brother, Petropolis, is dying.

At a terrifying height earthly dreams gutter,
An emerald star is flying:
Oh, if you are a star—sky and water's brother—
Your brother, Petropolis, is dying.

A monstrous ship at a terrifying height
Is borne swiftly, all sails flying.
O emerald star, in your splendid plight
Your brother, Petropolis, is dying.

Translucent spring has broken above the black Nevá,
Immortality's wax is melting.
Petropolis, your city—if you are a star—
Your brother, Petropolis, is dying.

(101, 87*)   March, 1918

12

When Moscow's feverish forum dies
And theaters' jaws gape open,
Returning the crowds to the squares
And the night,

There courses through its sumptuous streets
The liveliness of a midnight wake
And crowds of mourning revelers throng
Out of the maw of some divine abyss.

It is the common citizenry, incited by the Games,
Who are coming to bury the nocturnal sun,
Returning from the funeral feast
To the muffled hammering of hooves.

It's as if Herculáneum's resurrected anew:
A city sleeping in the moonlight glare
With its wretched market hovels
And mighty Doric columns.

(102, 88*)   May, 1918, Moscow

I3 *THE TWILIGHT OF FREEDOM*
(An Anthem)

Brothers, let us celebrate liberty's twilight,
The great and gloomy year.
Into the seething waters of the night
The cumbersome frame of nets is cast.
You're rising to times of oblivion
O sun, O justice, O people!

Let us prise the fateful load
That the people's leader assumes in tears.
And praise the twilight burden power bears,
Its insupportable goad.
He who has a heart must hear, O time,
Your ship as it sinks to the ocean floor.

We've pressed the swallows into battle legions,
And now the sun's concealed;
All the elements twitter and stir alive;
Through the nets, while the dusk lies thick,
The sun can't be seen and the earth's adrift.

So we might as well try setting sail:
Huge and clumsy creaks the turning wheel:
The earth's at sea. Men, be brave.
Like a plough it furrows the ocean wave,
And we'll still recall in Lethe's cold
That earth cost us a dozen heavens.

(103, 89*)   Early May, 1918, Moscow

I've acquired the craft of separating
In the unbraided laments of the night.
With oxen chewing and tedious waiting,
The city watch drags out the hour till light;
I revere the ritual of that night when cockerels crow,
When tear-stained eyes strained afar and long,
Assuming the burden of wayfarers' woe,
And women's weeping mingled with the Muses' song.

Who can know in this word called separation
What kind of parting mean the coming days,
And what bodes us in the cockerel's clamation
When on the Acropolis the fires blaze?
And in the dawn of some new age,
With the lazy oxen chewing in the stall,
Why the cock, the herald of the coming age,
Beats its wings on the city wall?

And I love the routine weaving-round,
The spindle's hum, the shuttle's click.
See where barefoot Delia, like swansdown,
Is borne toward us, flying on the wind.
Oh, the straitened basis of our lives!
What could be more wretched than the language of bliss?
Everything has been before and again will come to pass;
The instant of recognition is all we ever miss.

So be it: A transparent figure lies
On a clean dish of porcelain glaze
As a pegged-out squirrelskin dries;
Bent over wax, a young woman's gaze.
It's not for us to divine the Erebus of Greece:
For women, wax; for men, bronze armor's metal;
For us the dice are cast as we go forth to battle,
But women prophesy at their own decease.

(104, 90*)   1918

47

15

Heaviness and tenderness, you're sisters with the same device;
Bumblebees and wasps both suck the heavy rose;
Man dies, warm sand cools down,
And yesterday's sun is borne away on a black bier.

Ah, heavy honeycombs and tender nets!
I can more easily raise rocks than speak this name.
There's only one care I have left in the world:
The golden need to ease the burden of time.

Like darkened water I drink the murky air.
As time is turned by the plough, once the rose was earth.
In sluggish eddies, the tender roses' heavy spin;
The rose's heaviness and tenderness are twined in double
    wreaths.

(108, 93*)   March, 1920, Koktebel', Crimea.

16

Where night casts anchor
In the Zodiac's forsaken constellations,
Where are you flying to,
                        October's withered leaves,
Forgotten suckling babes of dark?
Why have you fallen from the tree of life?
Bethlehem for you is alien and strange,
Nor have you ever known a crib.

Alas, you leave no heirs behind;
A sexless bitchiness possesses you:
Childless you shall go down
Into your lamented graves;
And on the very brink of silence
Where no remembrance is kept by nature,
It's not to you the undying nations
Are condemned; they're fated for the stars.

(-, -*)   1920, Koktebel', Crimea

17

Take, for joy's sake, from these hands of mine
A little honey and a little sunlight
As the bees of Persephone once ordered us to do.

We cannot cast adrift an unmoored boat,
Nor hear a shadow shoed in fur,
Nor conquer fear in this tangled dreaming life.

All we have left to us are kisses,
Sheathed in down like tiny bees
That die as they scatter from the hive.

They rustle in the translucent recesses of the night,
Their homeland is Taigetos' tangled woods,
Their food is honeysuckle, time, and mint.

So take, for joy's sake, this wild gift of mine,
This uninviting dessicated necklet
Made of dead bees that once turned honey into sunlight.

(116, 102*)   November, 1920

18

In Petersburg we'll meet again
As though it was where we'd laid the sun to rest
And there we'll utter one first time
The word that's senseless but blessed.
In the black velvet of the Soviet night,
In the velvet of the universal void,
The beloved eyes of blessèd women still sing
And immortal flowers still bloom.

The wildcat capital arches its back,
On the bridge a sentinel stands watch.
Only a cuckoo car horn blares,
Through the dark its angry engine roars.
I don't need a permit for the night:
Sentinels don't frighten me;
For the senseless and blessèd word
I shall pray in the Soviet night.

I hear the theater's gentle rustle,
And the young girls' surprise;
A huge bouquet of immortal roses
Is held up by Aphrodite's arms.
We warm ourselves from boredom round a brazier fire,
Maybe after centuries have passed,
The beloved hands of blessèd women
Will gather our frail ashes at last.

Somewhere scarlet flowerbeds of stalls,
Sumptuous chests of drawers, the boxes round the walls,
And an officer like a clockwork doll;
Not for the vile and unctuous or the lowly soul. . . .
So, you might as well snuff out our lights
In the black velvet of the universal void;
The blessèd women's sloping shoulders still sing
But the nocturnal sun won't be seen by you.

(118, 99*)   November 25, 1920

19

Because I didn't dare hold off your embraces,
Because I've betrayed your tender salt lips,
I must await Acropolis:
—Oh, how I hate those weeping ancient beams.

The warriors of Greece set the Horse up in the dark,
Their serrated saws gnaw deep into the walls.
This drab dry bustle in the blood shall not be staunched—
You have no name, no sound and no likeness.

How dared I think that you'd return, how rash!
Why did I flee from you before I had to go?
Night had not dispersed, the cocks had not yet crowed,
The heated axes hadn't hacked into the wood.

Resin's oozed onto the walls like a tear
And the city feels its ribs as wooden beams,
But blood has flowed forward and surged up the steps
While the warriors have three times glimpsed a tempting
        dream.

Where is lovely Troy, the king's and Helen's home?
It shall be destroyed, Priam's lofty house of birds.
Arrows will fall in a dry wooden rain,
And other barbs will sprout, like a nutgrove, from the ground.

The last star's piercing jab is painlessly withdrawn
And like a gray swallow dawn will flap against the window,
And the slow day stirs, like an ox amid its straw,
And shakes itself from sleep in the rustling streets and squares.

(119, 103*)   December, 1920

20

Along with all the others
I want to serve you too,
And inflamed with jealousy
Through parched lips to prophesy.
The word itself can't slake
The thirst from which my dry lips ache,
But now without you once again
The tangled air's a void of pain.

I'm not jealous any longer,
But I want you now.
It's I who bring myself to bow
My head upon the block.
I shall not call you any longer
Either joy or love;
My blood has been changed
For something wild and strange.

If you wait another instant,
It's this I'll say to you:
It isn't joy but torment
That I find in you.
And, as if it were a crime,
What drags me back is this:
Your bitten and bewildered
Tender cherry lips.

Come back quickly to me
Without you I am scared,
I've never felt you so strongly.
And all that I desire
I see when I'm awake.
Anxious or in passion,
It's you I'm calling.

(122, 106*)   1920

2 I

I washed in the courtyard at night—
The firmament shone with coarse stars.
Like salt on an axhead the starlight,
The rain-butt is chilled to its brim.

The yard gates are locked up tight
And the earth, in all conscience, is grim.
Fresh canvas is a purer base for truth
Than you're likely to find elsewhere.

In the rain-butt a star melts like salt:
The freezing water is blacker,
Death cleaner, misfortune more bitter,
And the earth, though grimmer, is more just.

(126, 109*)   Autumn, 1921, Moscow

Winter for some is arak spirit and blue-eyed punch,
For others cinnamon and sparkling wine.
But some must carry the salty decrees
Of cruel stars into a smoke-filled hut.

A few warm droppings of chickens
And the witless warmth of sheep:
I'd give the lot for life (my need for care's so great)
And a sulphur match to keep me warm.

Look: my hand holds just an earthen flask
And the chirruping of the stars tickles my weak ear,
But through this wretched feather-down
You can't help loving yellow grass and warm loam,

Softly stroking fur or rustling in the straw,
Starving like an apple tree lagged against winter,
Being senselessly tenderly drawn to another,
Or fumbling blindly in space while you patiently wait.

Let conspirators flock through snow like sheep
And let the brittle snow crust squeak,
Winter for some is bitter smoke and wormwood at night rest,
For others the stern salt of triumphant griefs.

Oh, just to raise a lantern on a pole
And walk beneath the salt of stars while a dog runs on ahead,
And with a jugged rooster call at a fortune teller's home,
But the white, white snow chews my eyes till they ache.

(127, 110*)   1922

My age, wild beast, who dare
Deep into your pupils stare,
And ever use his blood to weld
Two centuries' spinal cords in one?
A jet of building blood springs
Through the throat from earthly things,
But the sluggard merely sways
On the brink of these new days.

A creature, as long as life persists,
Must bear its backbone and exist,
And a wave rolls and plays
Down invisible vertebrae.
Like a child's soft cartilage,
The era of the infant earth,
Life's brainpan has been offered up,
Like a sacrificial lamb.

To rip the very age from bondage
And with it found a newer world,
The intertwining joints of days
Need binding by the music of a flute.
It's the age that shakes the wave
With human longing, human grief,
And the adder in the grass
Breathes the age's golden measure.

And once again the buds will swell
And nature will explode in green,
But your spinal cord is snapped,
My wonderful but sorry age.
And with an idiotic grin
You gaze backward, weak and cruel,
Like a beast that once was supple
At the spoor you've left behind.

A jet of building blood springs forth
Through the throat from the things of earth
And like a feverish fish it flails
The warm gravel of the seas ashore.
And from a net of flying birds,
Off the blue soaking blocks and shards
Apathy streams, indifference pours
On that fatal wound of yours.

(135, 118*)   1923-36

24 THE FINDER OF A HORSESHOE
(A Pindaric fragment)

We look at woods and we say:
Here is a forest, for ships and for masts;
The pink pines
Stand free to their tops of bushy accretions,
They should creak in a storm
As do lone-standing stone pines
In the infuriated forestless air;
Beneath the salty heel of the wind the plumbline stands firm,
    driven sheer to the dancing deck,
And a seafarer
In the unfettered thirst of emptiness,
Dragging through the soaking hollows
    the fragile instrument of the surveyor,
Compares the rough surface of the seas
Against the attraction of the landward mass.
And inhaling the odor
Of resinous tears sweating out through the joints of the ship,
Admiring the decking,
Riveted and squared into bulkheads,
Not by the peaceful carpenter of Bethlehem but by another,
The father of voyages and seafarers' friend,
We say:
And they too once stood on dry land,
As uncomfortable as an ass's back,
At their tops oblivious of their roots
On a famous mountain ridge.
And they soughed beneath fresh torrential rains,
Unsuccessfully suggesting to heaven that their noble load
Be exchanged for a pinch of salt.

From what should we begin?
Everything splits and sways,
The air's a-tremor from comparisons.
No single word is better than any other,

The earth is buzzing with metaphor.
And light two-wheelers,
Garishly harnessed to flocks of straining birds,
Collapse in fragments,
Rivaling the snorting favorites of the tracks.

Thrice-blesséd is he who enshrines a name in song,
A song embellished by a name
Lives longer than all others;
It stands out among the rest by the frontlet on its brow,
That heals it from amnesia, from the stupefying smell;
Whether the closeness of a man
Or the odor exuded by a strong beast's coat,
Or simply the scent of savory rubbed between the palms.

Air can get as dark as water and all things in it swim like fish,
Thrusting the element past with their fins,
For it is solid, elastic, slightly warmed,
A crystal where wheels turn and horses shy,
The damp black soil of Neaira, each night turned up anew,
By pitchforks, tridents, mattocks, ploughs;
The air's worked over as thickly as the ground:
One can't get out from it, nor easily get in.

A rustle rushes through the trees like a green racket;
But the children play at five-stones with the vertebras of dead
        beasts,
And the fragile chronography of our times is drawing to a close.
Thank you for that which has been:
I myself went wrong, was mistaken, made an error in my
        calculations;
The era echoed like a golden orb,
Hollow, cast, not supported by anyone,
And responded "Yes" and "No" to each touch
As a child can answer equally:
"I'll give you an apple" or "I shall not give it to you,"
While his face is an accurate cast of his voice as he utters the
        words.

The sound continues to ring though the source of the sound has
    gone,
A horse lies in the dust and snorts in a sweat,
But the steep curve of its neck
Still retains remembrance of the race in its outstretched hooves
When there were not just four,
But as many hooves as stones in the road,
Redoubled in four dimensions
By the number of thuds on the ground of the racehorse seething
    with heat.
Thus
The finder of the horseshoe
Blows the dust off it
And polishes it with wool till it shines,
Then
He hangs it on his door
For it to rest,
And to free it from the need to strike sparks from flint.
Human lips with nothing more to say
Retain the shape of their last uttered word,
And a sense of heaviness stays in the hand
Though a jug being carried home has half spilled over.

That which I'm saying now is not me speaking
But has been dug from the earth like grains of fossilized wheat.
Some stamp coins with lions,
Others stamp them with heads;
All kinds of copper, bronze, and gold wafers,
Equally honored, lie in the earth.
The age has tried to chew them and left on each the clench of its
    teeth.
Time clips me like a coin
And there isn't enough of me left for myself.

(136, 119*)   Moscow, 1923

And star speaks unto star
M. LERMONTOV

A mighty junction of star with star,
The flinty path in an older song
In language of flint and air combined:
Flint meets water and ring joins horseshoe;
On the soft shale of the clouds
A milky slate-gray sketch is drawn:
Not the discipleship of worlds
But the delirious dreams of mooning sheep.

Amid thick night we standing sleep
Beneath a cozy sheepskin cap.
To its source the stream burbles back
Like a warbler, chain or speech.
Here terror writes, here writes displacement
In a milky lead-pencil hand,
And here is shaped a rough-draft version
Of running water's own disciples.

The steeply sloping goats' home cities
Are a mighty layering of flints:
But in any case the mountain ridges
Are churches and settlements of sheep.
The overhanging cliff face preaches
While time tempers and water teaches
And the translucent glades of air
With all things have long been filled.

Like a dead hornet from beside a hive
The many-hued day is swept off in scorn,
And night, the she-kite, carries off
The burning chalk and feeds the slate.
From the iconoclastic board

Wipe away the day's impressions
And shake those transparent apparitions
Like a fledgling from the hands.

The fruit swelled up. The grapes grew ripe.
The day was stormy as days can be.
A friendly game of knucklebones. At noon,
The coats of vicious sheepdogs;
Like garbage from the icy heights,
The seamy side of fresh green imagery,
Hungry water flows and turns
And plays about like a tiny beast.

And like a spider crawls to me,
Where each join is spattered by the moon;
On a shuddering steep-pitched slope
I hear the juddering screech of slate:
Is it your voices, oh my memory,
Playing teacher as they tear the night
And hunting with slate pencils through the woods,
Scavenging from the beaks of birds?

It's only from the voice we'll know
That there was scratching and conflict there;
So we draw the hard pencil in the one direction
Indicated by the voice.
I tear the night, the burning chalk,
For the sake of an instantaneous record.
I change for noise the song of arrows
And for order the clatter of bustards' wings.

Who am I? Not a real stone mason,
No shipwright I; I don't roof buildings,
I'm a double-dealer with a double soul,
The friend of night, the day's assailant.
Blesséd be he who first dubbed flint
The disciple of running water.
Blesséd be he who thongs first tied
To the feet of hills and on firm ground.

And now I study the rough-hewn ledger
Of the scratches made in the slate-pencil summer:
The language of flint and air combined
With a stratum of darkness and a stratum of light.
And I want to place my fingers
In the flinty path from the older song
As in a lesion, binding, joining
Flint to water, ring to horseshoe.

(137, 120*)   1923

27

Like summer lightning a life fell away,
As an eyelash into a tumbler falls,
Life lied to the bitter end:
I don't accuse, I don't defend.

Do you want an apple in the night?
Do you want hot honey, fresh and light?
Do you want me to take your boots off,
To lift you like a fleck of fluff?

Angel clad in a golden fleece
Standing in a web of light,
The lamplight plays upon your face
And lights the shoulders I've embraced.

Will a cat leaping up before us,
Bounding off like a wild hare,
Really seal the way ahead of us
When it falls from sight somewhere?

Your flushed lips puckered and trembled
As you poured your son his tea;
You rambled on to him and me,
You gabbled and dissembled.

As you stuttered foolishness,
Lied and smiled with tenderness:
A blush flooded your face
With clumsy beauty and awkward grace.

Behind a tower on a palace,
Behind the garden cuckoospit;
In that beyond-the-eyelid life
You will surely be my wife.

So putting on dry felt boots
And donning golden sheepskin coats,
Let us set off hand in hand
Down the same road to the distant land,

Without a backward glance, no hindrance and no fear,
Toward that shimmering frontier:
Where from dusk to the pre-dawn glow
Streetlamps with light overflow. . . .

(198, 128*)   January, 1925

28

On police station watermarked paper—
Night has choked on its sticklebacked fish—
Stars sing in chorus and red-tape worms
Ceaselessly write their Prolexkult reports.

No matter how you stars want to shine
First apply on the proper dotted line;
We're sure to renew your permission
For shining or writing or extinction.

(219,—*)   October, 1930

I returned to my city, familiar as tears,
As veins, as mumps from childhood years.

You've returned here, so swallow as quick as you can
The cod-liver oil of Leningrad's riverside lamps.

Recognize when you can December's brief day:
Egg yolk folded into its ominous tar.

Petersburg, I don't yet want to die:
You have the numbers of my telephones.

Petersburg, I have addresses still
Where I can raise the voices of the dead.

I live on the backstairs and the doorbell buzz
Strikes me in the temple and tears at my flesh.

And all night long I await those dear guests of yours,
Rattling, like manacles, the chains on the doors.

(221, 144*)   December, 1930, Leningrad

30

I'll tell you bluntly
One last time:
It's only maddening cherry brandy,
Angel mine.

Where the Greeks saw just their raped
Beauty's fame,
Through black holes at me there gaped
Nought but shame.

But the Greeks hauled Helen home
In their ships.
Here a smudge of salty foam
Flecks my lips.

What rubs my lips and leaves no trace?
—Vacancy.
What thrusts a V-sign in my face?
—Vagrancy.

Quickly, wholly, or slowly as a snail,
All the same,
Mary, angel, drink your cocktail,
Down your wine.

I'll tell you bluntly
One last time:
It's only maddening cherry brandy,
Angel mine.

(226, 147*)

31

For the resounding valor of millenia to come,
For the high-sounding name of the great human race,
I've cut myself off from honor and joy
At my ancestors' feast, from my cup and my place.

The wolf-hound century leaps at my throat
But it isn't wolf's blood that flows through my veins,
You'd do better to shove me, like a cap, up the sleeve
Of the hot fur coat of Siberia's plains

Where I needn't see cowards or glutinous muck
Or bloody bones ground within wheels,
So the primeval splendor of the blue Arctic fox
Will gleam for me all the night long.

Lead me off in the night where the Yenisei flows,
Where the pines reach up to the stars,
Because it's not wolf's blood that flows through my veins
And my mouth has been twisted by lies.

(227, 149*)   March 17-28, 1931

32

A certain Alexander Herzovich,
A minor Jewish musician,
Played Schubert sonatas day and night
With diamond-like precision.

To music he was a martyr,
Learning his lieder by rote,
He practised the same sonata
Till he knew every fiddling half note.

So what, Alexander Herzovich,
It was dark outside long ago,
Chuck it, Alexander Scherzovitch!
What you're up to we don't wish to know.

So long as snow is hard at the edge,
So what if some Italian wench
Follows Schubert on a sledge,
So what, Alex Herzawrench?

It's not so hard for us to die
To mournful music's sad refrain.
It's a black fur coat being put away
On a hanger till winter comes again.

That's all, Alexander Herzovich,
It was played out long ago.
Chuck it, Alexander Scherzovitch,
What you're up to we don't wish to know.

(228, 150*)   March 27, 1931

My eyelashes sting and a tear has welled up in my heart.
I feel without fear what will come; what's to come is a storm,
And somebody strange is in a hurry to have me forgotten:
It's stifling, yet I'd give my life just to live.

I rise from my plank bunk at the very first sound,
Wildly and drowsily gazing around;
As someone in canvas drab rasps out a prison song
And dawn rises in a stripe above the old stockade.

(229, 148*)   March, 1931, Moscow

34

I drink to military asters, to all that I'm censured about,
To the Aristo's fur coat, to asthma, to the jaundiced Petersburg
    day,
To the music of pines in Savoie, petrol on the Champs-Elysées.
To roses in a Rolls-Royce saloon, to Parisian pictures' oil paint.

I drink to the surf of Biscay, to a jug of cream from the Alps,
To English girls' redheaded hauteur, and distant colonial
    quinine;
I drink but still have to choose between wines:
Sparkling Asti Spumante or Chateauneuf-du-Pape.

(233, —*)   April 11, 1931

Still far from patriarch or sage,
I'm still a half-respected age.
I still get cursed behind my back
In the savage tongue of tramcar rows,
Possessed of neither rhyme nor sense,
"What a so-and-so!" Oh, I apologize,
But in my heart don't mend my ways.

If you think, you'd not believe yourself,
What ties you to the world is rubbish:
A midnight key to someone's flat,
A silver coin in your pocket
And the celluloid of a detective film.

I rush like a puppy to the phone
Every hysterical time it rings:
A Polish voice saying: "Tzank you, Sur,"
A soft reproach from another town,
Some obligation unfulfilled.

You wonder what you dare to like
Amid these tricks and fireworks.
You boil over: but it won't go away—
The meddling hands of idleness—
Please get a light from them, not me.

I sometimes laugh and sometimes try
To play the gentleman with white-handled walking stick;
I hear sonatas in alleyways,
I lick my lips at hawker's trays,
I leaf through books in blocky entranceways
And do not live, yet seem to live.

I'll visit reporters and sparrows,
I'll go to a street photographer:

In no time he'll fish from a bucket
An adequate likeness of me
Against Shah Mountain's lilac cone.

And sometimes I run off on errands
To airless cellars filled with steam
Where Chinamen, honest and clean,
Use chopsticks to pick at paste balls
And drink vodka like swallows from the Yang-Tze.

And I love the squeaking trams' departures
And the asphalt's Astrakhan caviar
All covered in straw like matting;
It reminds me of baskets of Asti
And the ostrich fans of building-yard junk
When Leninist houses first rise.

I enter puppet-theater museums
Where opulent Rembrandts swell,
Now glazed like Cordova leather
I marvel at Titian's horned miters
And Tintoretto's bright tints I admire
For their myriad screaming parakeets. . . .

But how I'd love to speak my mind,
To play the fool, to spit out truth,
Send spleen to the dogs, to the devil, to hell,
Take someone's arm and say, "Be so kind,
I think your way lies the same as mine."

(251, 155*)   May-September, 1931, Moscow

TO THE GERMAN LANGUAGE

36

Ruining myself, contradicting myself,
As a moth flies into a midnight flame,
I want to leave the Russian language behind
For all that I owe it on endless credit.

There's praise between us without flattery,
And point-blank friendship without hypocrisy;
But let's learn a seriousness and honor
From an alien family in the West.

Poetry can find a use for storms:
I remember a German officer,
His sword hilt entwined in roses
And on his lips the name of Ceres.

Frankfurt's fathers still scarcely stirred,
As yet of Goethe there was no word,
As hymns were being composed, and horses pranced
And on the spot, like letters, danced.

Tell me, my friends, in what Valhalla
You and I cracked nuts together,
What liberties were ours and whether
You placed milestones along my path?

And straight from the page of the Almanach,
From its incunabulous novelty,
You ran bravely down into the grave
As if to the cellar for a mug of Moselle.

This foreign tongue shall be a membrane for me;
And long before I dared be born,
I was a letter, I was a grape of verse,
I was a book you dream before you write.

When I still slept without form or shape,
I was forced awake by friendship, like a shot.
Ah, Nachtigall, my god, grant me Pylades' fate.
Or tear out my tongue; I need it not.

God Nachtigall, I'm still being drafted to assist
Those on new-hatched plagues and seven-year carnage bent.
Sound is compressed; words rebel and hiss,
But you are living and with you I'm content.

(266, 169*)   August 8-12, 1932

ARIOSTO [Variation]

37

In Europe it is cold; in Italy it's dark,
Power is repulsive as were the barber's hands.
Oh, if only we could open, as quickly as can be,
A broad window overlooking the Adriatic Sea.

Bees are humming noisily above the wild musk rose
And a muscled cricket clatters amid the southern steppe,
The wingéd horse's horseshoes weigh him down
And the hourglass sands glint both gold and yellow.

In the cicadas' strident tongue there's a captivating blend
Of Pushkin's ennui and Mediterranean hubris;
Like clinging ivy, all-grasping, grabbing all,
Most manfully he lies and whirls with wild Orlando.

The hourglass has a golden yellow glint,
A muscled cricket clatters amid the midday steppe,
And wild Orlando flies off for the moon. . . . .

Gentle Ariosto, emissary fox,
Hundred year aloe, wind-sailor, flowering fern,
You listened to the buntings' voices on the moon
And provided learned counsel at the fishes' court.

O lizard city, where there's not a soul alive,
O stale Ferrara, you gave birth to sons like this
From witch and judge and bound them with a chain,
And in a backward province
                    his redhead mind rose like the sun.

At the butcher's bloody stall we register surprise
At a soundly sleeping child behind a net of flies
At a lamb upon a hillside, and on an ass a monk,
At the soldiers of the Duke, gone slightly imbecile
From plague, from garlic, from all the wine they've drunk,
And fresh as is the dawn, the loss causes us surprise.

(268, 170*)   May 4-6, 1933, Stary Krym (Old Crimea)
                     1936, Voronezh

38

A cold spring in starving Old Crimea.
As it was in Wrangel's time, its same old guilty air.
Sheepdogs in the backyards, patches on its tatters,
The same old gray and gnawing smoke.

The distracted distance is still as beautiful,
The trees, with buds now swelling just a little,
They stand like strangers; and the almond bloom
Arouses pity for its rashness of the day before,

Nature won't recognize its features as its own;
And, fearsome shadows cast from the Kuban and Ukraine,
As if wearing silent slippers, the starving peasants
Watch the garden gate but do not touch the chain.

(271, -*)

May, 1933
Stary Krym (Old Crimea)

39

The apartment's as quiet as paper,
Empty, without any schemes,
You can hear the water gurgle
Through the radiator pipes in the walls.

My property is completely in order,
My phone squats still like a frog,
But my scandalized rags and possessions
Beg to get out like a dog.

The accursed walls are too thin
But there's nowhere left now to run,
And I'm forced to play someone strange tunes,
Like some fool who hums through a comb.

And cruder than songs students sing,
Far coarser than a Komsomol cell,
I teach hangmen how to chirrup
Although they still cannot spell;

Ration books are now all I read,
Demagogues' speeches are all I hear,
A lullaby of threats is what I sing
To teach the kulak's kid to fear.

Some honest portrayer or other,
Some carder of collective-farm flax,
Some incestuous, ink-mixing father
Doesn't want trouble like that.

Some honest betrayer or other,
Parboiled, like salt, in the Purge,
Supporter of family and mother,
Swats moths like that when he's urged . . .

And there's so much torturing malice
Concealed in every remark,
As if Nekrassov's old mallet
Was hammering nails in the dark.

Let's use you to get this thing started,
After seventy years of this noose,
It's high time, you scruffy old bastard,
You were stumping the streets in your boots.

Not Hippocrene's spring but one faster,
An ancient current of fear,
Will burst through the jerry-built plaster
Of the vicious home I have here.

(272, -*)

November, 1933,
Moscow, Furmanov Lane

40 *FROM OTTAVE*

VII

Both Schubert on the waters and Mozart in the din of birds,
And Goethe whistling down a winding path,
And even Hamlet, who thought with timorous steps,
All felt the people's pulse and trusted in the crowd.
As the whisper perhaps evolved before lips,
And leaves spun and circled long before there were trees,
So those, it may be, whom our experience endows,
Before such experience have acquired their traits.

(281, 171*)   January, 1934, Moscow

VIII

The fretted paw of a maple leaf
Bathes in the corners of circles,
And pictures can be drawn on walls
With specks of dust from a butterfly.
There are such things as living mosques,
And it's only now I realize
That maybe we are Hagia Sophia
With a countless quantity of eyes.

(282, -*)   November, 1933 - January, 1934, Moscow

IX

Tell me, draftsman of the desert,
Surveyor of the sinking sands:
Is the unrestraint of lines
Really stronger than the blowing winds?
—I'm not concerned with the way he shivers
From those Judaean woes of his—
He models what he learns from blab,
And it's blab from what he's learned he drinks.

(283, -*)   November, 1933, Moscow

41

We live without feeling beneath us firm ground,
At ten feet away you can't hear the sound

Of any words but "the wild man in the Kremlin,
Slayer of peasants and soul-strangling gremlin."

Each thick finger of his is as fat as a worm,
To his ten-ton words we all have to listen,

His cockroach whiskers flicker and squirm
And his shining thigh-boots shimmer and glisten.

Surrounding himself by scrawny-necked lords,
He plays on his servile half-human hordes

Some mewl, some grizzle, some moan,
Prodded by him, scourging us till we groan.

Like horseshoes he hammers out law after law
Slamming some in the gut and some in the eye,
And some in the balls and some in the jaw;

At each execution, he belches his best
This Caucasian hero with his broad tribesman's chest.

(286, -*)   October (?), 1933

42

What is the name of this street?
Mandelstam Street.
What the hell kind of name is that?
No matter how you turn it round,
It has a crooked sound, it isn't straight.

There wasn't much about him straight,
His attitudes weren't lily-white.
And that's why this street
Or better still, this hole
Was given its name after him:
This Mandelstam.

(303, -*)   April 1935, Voronezh

The day was five-headed. For five days and five nights;
Hunched up, I took pride in space for rising on yeast;
Sleep was older than hearing or rumor;
                Rumor older than sleep—fused yet on guard;
And behind us the highway was borne on coachdrivers' reins.

The day was five-headed and, catching plague from the dance,
The cavalry rode while on foot tramped the black-coated horde:
With power's aorta dilated, in the northern white nights—
    no, in knives,
The eye turned into conifer pith.

Oh, an inch! Oh give me a needle's eyeful of blue sea!
So the escort's double-watch would sweep past with sails flying
Familiar sweet legend of Russia! Wooden spoon, here I am!
Where are you three fine lads from the secret police's iron gates?

Keeping Pushkin's fine goods from parasites' hands,
A tribe of young lovers of gleaming-toothed verse,
The scholars of Pushkin, are schooled with their greatcoats and
    guns;
Oh, give me an inch, a needle's eyeful of blue sea!

Our train was bound for the Urals. A talking Chapayev
From a post-silent movie leaped into our wide-open mouths;
Behind a timber fence, on a sheet of film,
To die and leap back onto his horse.

(313, -*)   June, 1935, Voronezh

44

Wave to wave the comber runs, breaking the backs of waves,
In fettered anguish leaping at the moon
And the young janissaries' ocean deeps
—The sleepless breakers' capital—
Curve and tumble and carve a moat in sand.

As if through the murky cotton air
Loom the battlements of an unbuilt wall,
And from their foaming ladders fall
The suspicious sultan's soldiery—besmirched and torn apart—
While sullen eunuchs distribute poison all about.

(319, -*)   July, 1935, Voronezh

45

With them and not with you or me
The power of family endings lies:
The reed is porous and singing with their air,
And gratefully the snails of human lips
Pull on their breathing gravity.

They have no name. Enter their sinews
And you will be their principalities' heir,
And for people, for their living hearts,
Stumbling through their every fork and turn,
You'll portray their great content
And what they're tortured by in ebbs and flows.

(328, -*)   December 9-27, 1937, Voronezh

46

Where is that bound and fettered groan?
Where is Prometheus, the crag's buttress and support?
And where is the kite and yellow-gazing slash
Of talons flying out from beneath its brow?

It cannot come again; tragedy has no return,
But these threatening lips bring us to the very quick
Of Aeschylus' essential burden, and to the wood
Chopped away by Sophocles.

He is the echo and the greeting, the milestone, no—the plough;
The airy stone-built theater of our growing times
Has risen to its feet; and we all want to glimpse
All those born, destroyed, and dispossessed of death.

(356, 202*)   January 19 - February 4, 1937, Voronezh

VERSES ON THE UNKNOWN SOLDIER

(1)

Let this air be called as a witness:
The long-range heart that it has,
And in dugouts, omnivorous and active
Is the ocean, windowless stuff.

How denunciatory these stars are, for all that:
They need to see all (but what for?)
In condemning the judge and the witness
To the ocean, windowless stuff.

The rain recalls, like an unwelcoming farmer,
And the anonymous manna it sows,
The forests of crosses branding
The ocean or formation of soldiers.

Sickly cold folk shall keep existing,
Keep killing, keep chilling, keep starving,
While under his illustrious tombstone
The unknown soldier is laid.

Teach me, puny sick swallow,
Now you've forgotten how to fly
How I can, rudderless, wingless,
Cope with that tomb in the sky.

And for the poet, Mikhail Lérmontov,
I'll provide you the strictest account
Of how the grave trains the round-shouldered
And the air pocket sucks us all down.

March 3, 1937, Voronezh

Like shivering clusters of grapes
These worlds are a threat to us here,
And the golden constellations of stars,
Fatty tent-tops of constellations reaching out,
Hang overhead like kidnapped cities,
Like gold slips of the tongue, slanders of gold,
Like berries of poisonous cold.

(3)

Through the ether, decimalized to the tenth place,
The light of speeds ground down to a beam
Starts a number that's been turned transparent
By light's pain and a moleful of noughts.

Beyond the field of fields a newer field
Flies like a triangular crane:
The news flies down its beam of dusted light,
And it's still light from yesterday's battle.

The news flies down its beam of dusted light:
It's not Leipzig, not Waterloo
Nor the Battle of the Nations but something new,
It'll make the light brighter than light.

In the depths of the black marble oyster,
The embers of Austerlitz gutter:
A Mediterranean swallow squints its eyes
And the plague sands of Egypt get clogged.

(4)

An Arabian mess and a muddle,
The light of speeds honed into a beam—
And with its slanted soles,
A ray balances on my retina;

Millions of dead slaughtered wholesale
Have trampled a path in the void,
Good night and best wishes to all of them
On behalf of the strongholds underground.

Oh, unbribable sky of trench warfare,
Sky of massive wholesale deaths,
For you and by you, the whole of you,
I rush with my lips through the dark,

Past foxholes, embankments, and rubble-heaps,
Past which there loitered, shedding gloom,
The miserable grim pock-marked genius
And humble spirit of burst-open tombs.

(5)

The infantry knows how to die,
And night choirs know how to sing,
At soldier Schweik's stub-snouted smile,
At Don Quixote's bird-beaked lance
And at the knight's birdlike metatarsus.
Now the cripple makes friends with the human:
For them both there's work to be found
And a brood of crutches stumps round
The century's furthest-flung fringes,
Calling the globe to the comradeship of war.

(6)

Is it for this the skull grows wide
And from temple to temple fills the brow,
To stop the sockets of its eyes
From being filled with soldiery?
The skull grows wide from life,
From temple to temple to fill the brow;
It teases itself with the neatness of its seams,

Achieving clarity through comprehension's dome,
Bubbling with thought and dreaming of itself,
Cups of cups and fatherland's country
A cap picked out with star-spangled ribs—
Shakespeare's father—good fortune's cap.

(7)

Ash-tree clarity, sycamore vision,
Slightly blushing, rush back to their home,
As if casting spells with fits of fainting
On both heavens with their fading fire.

We have as allies only what's superfluous,
Soundings ahead touch no bottom nor abyss,
And to fight for just breathing space enough
Is the greatest glory of them all.

Was it for this that the package was prepared
Of attraction in empty space?
So that the white stars might hasten back,
Slightly reddened, rushing to their home?

And using my semi-comatose existence
To cast a spell on my own consciousness,
Can I choose not to sup this mixture?
Must I eat my head under fire?

Can you, stepmother from the camp of stars,
Sense the night that's coming now and later?

(8)

The aortas swell up with blood
And a whisper sounds down the rows:
"I was born in eighteen ninety-four,
No, in eighteen ninety-two. . . ."

94

And squashing the worn-out year of my birth
In my fist with the crowd and the herd
I whisper through bloodless lips:
"I was born in the night of the second and the third
Of January in the eighteen ninety-first
Untrustworthy year, and the centuries
Surround me with fire."

February - March, 1937,
Voronezh/Savëlovo

(362, -*)

48

The breaches of round bays, the gravel and the blue
And a slow sail, continued by a cloud:
I'm parted from you all I scarce appreciated.
Longer than organ fugues, the false-haired grass
Of the seas is bitter—and smacks of the long lie.
The head whirls from iron tenderness
And rust gnaws little by little at the sloping shore . . .
Why do I lay my head on other sands?
You, the throaty Ural, the heavy-shouldered Volga
Or these flat lands, are the only rights I have,
And I must breathe them still with a heavy heart.

(366, 206*)   February 4, 1937, Voronezh

49

I'll say it in draft in a whisper
Since we cannot speak openly yet:
The game of irrational heaven
Is attained via experience and sweat.

Beneath the temporary sky of purgatory
We frequently fail to recall
That this happy heaven-roofed depository
Is a flexible lifetime home.

(376, 214*)   March 9, 1937, Voronezh

50

Stooping involuntarily to the empty ground
With a gently hobbling gait she goes,
Slightly ahead of her faster friends,
What involves her, drags her down
Is the cramped freedom of her inspiring handicap,
And in her very limp it seems
A clear conjecture seeks to be delayed:
That this springtime weather is for us
The primal mother of the vault of death,
And this beginning shall forever be renewed.

There are some women who are kin to the raw earth,
Whose every pace is resonant with weeping;
To accompany the dead and be the first
To greet the resurrected is their vocation.
To plead caresses from them would be a crime
And to part with them is more than one can bear.
Today an angel, tomorrow a worm in the tomb,
The next day just an outline, nothing more.
What's been—a step—will be one step beyond our reach.
Flowers are immortal, heaven a single whole,
And what shall be is nothing but a promise.

(394, 223-224*)   May 4, 1937, Voronezh

First Lines and Brief Notes

1. Hagia Sophia: it was at this place (Hagia Sophia) ....

   Hagia Sophia: Church of the Holy Wisdom, Constantinople, one of the finest models of Byzantine architecture, built for Emperor Justinian I (A.D. 527-63). The poem illustrates Mandelstam's Acmeist theories.

2. The idle life has sent us insane ....

   Written in response to a poem by Anna Akhmatova (1899-1966): "We are all revelers and sluts. . . ." The last stanza refers to Georgii Ivanov (1894-1955), Acmeist poet.

3. There are orioles in the forests and the only real measure ....
   The poem imitates Graeco-Roman verse, particularly the bucolic eclogue. *Tonic verse*: also used of Russian prosody.

4. The bread is poisoned and the air's drunk dry ......

   Appears to have been written in the light of the expedition to Africa by Nikolai Gumilyov, Akhmatova's husband and one of the leading Acmeist poets. Gumilyov may have been the singer referred to in the last line of the final stanza.

5. Insomnia. Homer. Tautly swelling sails............

The language of the original is charged with an atmosphere of half-sleep. *The Catalogue of Ships*, Illiad, ii., describes the mustering of the Greek battlefleet against Troy.

6. In the polyphony of young girls' choirs ....

To the Russian poetess Marina Tsvetayeva (1892-1941), with whom Mandelstam first visited Moscow in 1915. *Note*: Much of the late mediaeval architecture in the Moscow Kremlin was designed by North Italian architects.

7. In a sledge packed deep in straw we lurched ....

To Marina Tsvetayeva (1892-1941). *Uglich*: city on the Volga, north of Moscow where Tsarevich (Crown Prince) Dimitry was murdered at the instigation of Boris Godunov in 1591. *Three meetings*: probably between Mandelstam and Tsvetayeva, but Cf. old Russian saying: Two Romes have fallen, the third (i.e., Moscow) stands, and a fourth is not to be. Note: deliberate confusion of the poet's identity.

8. When, sweet Salome, you can't sleep in your huge room (Salome) ....

To Salomeia Andronikova. The Russian original plays on the name Salome and its homophones, the Russian words for straw, insomnia, etcetera. *Eleonora, Ligeia*: Edgar Allan Poe's two heroines whose existence continued beyond the grave; *Seraphite*: a similar heroine of Balzac.

9. This night is beyond repair ....

The black sun: here, eclipse at the Crucifixion. Yellow sun:
see notes on No. 10. Like himself, his mother had broken
free of traditional Judaism. Judaeans . . . no priests left to
their race: emancipated Jews.

10. Among the priests and elders, the young Levite....

He: A.V. Kartashev (1875-1960), Minister for Religious
Affairs in Kerensky's Provisional Government of 1917. The
poem compares the two Revolutions with the story of the
Crucifixion. Yellow: for Mandelstam, yellow or gold, in
combination with black, were evocative of his Jewish
heritage.

11. At a terrifying height, a wandering fire ....

Petropolis: Petersburg (present-day Leningrad), abandoned
as capital in 1918. Star: probably the Pole Star, a common
symbol for Petersburg. Sky and water's brother: Mandel-
stam's epithet for the ship-weathervane on the spire of the
Admiralty, Petersburg's focal point.

12. When Moscow's feverish forum dies................

The theater is probably the Bolshoi. Mandelstam moved to
Moscow in March, 1918.

13. Brothers, let us celebrate liberty's twilight (The
Twilight of Freedom) ....

Readers should be cautioned against reading into this an
indictment of the October Revolution. The people's leader:
Lenin. Swallows: possibly the Russian people. The last
stanza, Cf. Tennyson's Ulysses.

14. I've acquired the craft of separating (Tristia) ....

Compare Ovid's *Tristia*, where the Roman poet describes his last night in Rome before banishment to the shores of the Black Sea. *As a pegged-out squirrelskin dries*: concealed quote from a poem by Anna Akhmatova, on the subject of divination by wax droplets in water.

15. Heaviness and tenderness, you're sisters with the same device ....

Yesterday's sun: the poet Alexander Pushkin (1799-1837). *This name*: Undeciphered, though feminine in the Russian original. *The plough*: Elsewhere, Mandelstam refers to the plough of poetry bursting asunder the strata of time.

16. Where night casts anchor ....

One of his "lost" Civil War poems, first printed in *Novoe Russkoe Slovo*, a Russian emigré journal, in April, 1971. Mandelstam was briefly jailed by the Whites shortly after writing the poem. *October's withered leaves*: more probably the Whites than the Communists.

17. Take for joy's sake from these hands of mine ....

Probably written to Olga Arbenina, an actress at the Mikhailovsky Theater, Petrograd. The *bees* probably symbolize words, and the *necklet* (line 14) is of words, i.e. the poem.

18. In Petersburg we'll meet again ....

Possibly written to Olga Arbenina. *We had interred the sun*: possibly a reference to Pushkin. *The word*: Cf. Akhmatova's "royal word," the poetic word.

19. Because I didn't dare hold off your embraces, ...

To Olga Arbenina. Based on Book IV of the Odyssey. Deliberate confusion of the poet's identity, as in No. 6. *House of birds*: palace.

20. Along with all the others..........................

To Olga Arbenina. Many of his poems written late in 1920 were dedicated to her.

21. I washed in the courtyard at night..................

The first poem in which Mandelstam completely discarded classical imagery. Typical of the verse he wrote in the period 1921-25, but atypically clear in its meaning.

22. Winter for some is arak spirit and blue-eyed punch ....

Arak: anis-based spirit in wide use throughout the Levant. *Blue-eyed punch*: blue flames on the surface of punch.

23. My age, wild beast, who dare (The Age)............

In Russian, "age" and "century" may be expressed by the same word. Readers should not assume that the poet is expressing resentment for the Revolution (see lines 8, 19-20).

24. We look at woods and we say (The Finder of a Horseshoe)..

A premonition of his five-year poetic silence. *The father of voyages*: Peter the Great. *Neaira*: probably the wife of Hyperion, symbol of unploughed land.

25. A mighty junction of star with star (The Ode on Slate) . . .

The title recalls the last poems by the poet Derzhavin (1743-1816), which were written on slate. *The flinty path from an older song*: reference to a poem by Mikhail Lermontov (1814-41).

26. Again the discordances of war . . . .

A long incomplete poem, in pacifist mode. *Nucleus of a storm*: the Russian word *yabloko* can mean apple (and here "apple of discord"), eyeball, eye, or nucleus. *Power of the few*: supporters of the Tsar. *Human birds* i.e., pilots.

27. Like summer lightning, a life fell away . . . .

To Olga Vaksel'. In 1925, Mandelstam was briefly but deeply in love with her, in a relationship which threatened to wreck his marriage. Probably his last poem for five years (1925-30).

28. On police station watermarked paper . . . .

Written shortly after the Armenian cycle. *Prolexkult*: Russian "RAPPortichki," pun on the word for police report and RAPP: Russian Association of Proletarian Poets, a later blossoming of the famous Proletkult poets, RAPP was particularly hostile to Mandelstam, and enjoyed official support for a while.

29. I returned to my city, familiar as tears (Leningrad). . . . . . .

Written during his last attempt to settle in Leningrad again. *Dear guests of yours*: "dear guests" was a euphemism for the political police.

30. I'll tell you bluntly ....

Contrast between the success of the Greek expedition
against Troy and the fatuousness of Mandelstam's own
existence at this period.

31. For the resounding valor of millenia to come ....

This poem, published in the Soviet (1973) edition of Man-
delstam's verse, caused problems for the poet in the early
nineteen thirties, perhaps due to the poem's last line.

32. A certain Alexander Herzovich.....................

Italian wench: probably Angelina Bosio (1830-59), Italian
soprano, about whose death in Petersburg Mandelstam at
one time intended to write a novel.

33. My eyelashes sting and a tear has welled up in my
      heart...

This poem was written when attacks on Mandelstam in the
press were at a lull, but after he had been told by writers'
union officials he was not wanted in Leningrad.

34. I drink to military asters, to all that I'm censured
      about ....

This poem anticipates the wave of criticism brought down
on Mandelstam as a "bourgeois internal emigre." It was not
published in his lifetime. *Military asters*: either military
decorations or the gold braid of epaulettes. The similes all
evoke the Western bourgeois world no longer accessible
to Soviet citizens as the right to travel abroad disap-
peared.

35. Still far from patriarch or sage.....................

The first stanza carries echoes of Mandelstam's theory of predetermination. *Shah mountain*: probably the cutout mountain backcloth frequently used by cheap studio photographers. *Leninist houses*: low-cost housing projects in Moscow of the period.

36. Ruining myself, contradicting myself (To the German Language)................................

To B.S. Kuzmin (1903-73), Soviet biologist, and close friend. *A German officer*: Ewald Christian von Kleist (1715-59), German poet, officer in the Prussian Army, killed during the Seven Years' War. Von Kleist printed verse in the German almanacs of his period. *Pylades*: Greek hero whose friendship with Orestes was legendary.

37. In Europe it is cold; in Italy it's dark (Ariosto) [Variation]..

Orlando: the wild, redheaded hero of an epic verse novel by Ludovico Ariosto (1474-1533), Italian poet, son of a judge, diplomat in the service of the Dukes of Ferrara. Torquatio Tasso (1544-95), Italian poet, was bound to a chain in a lunatic asylum for seven years for attacking the Duke of Ferrara. The *barber*: Peter the Great, who shaved the beards off his nobles, and built St. Petersburg as "a window overlooking Europe." *A muscled cricket*: elsewhere, Mandelstam refers to Sappho's poetic language as the noise of a muscled cricket.

38. A cold spring in starving Old Crimea...............

On the famine of 1932-33. The Mandelstams spent the spring of 1933 in the Crimea's ancient capital, Stary Krym

(Old Crimea). *Wrangel*: White Guard general who had operated out of the Crimea in the Civil War, 1919-20. *The Kuban' and Ukraine*: normally the granaries of the Soviet Union.

39. The apartment's as quiet as paper ....

The Mandelstams' period in this apartment was one of the more unpleasant periods in their nomadic life. The reading of *ration books* aloud: joke indulged in by Mandelstam. *Nekrasov's mallet*: Nikolai Nekrasov (1821-77), Russian poet.

40. Both Schubert on the waters and Mozart in the din
     of birds (From Ottave) ....

The din of birds: reference to the Magic Flute. The last four lines in Ottava VII are a key to Mandelstam's ideas on predetermination, Cf. Nos. 24, 34.

41. We live without feeling beneath us firm ground...

Epigrammatic poem about Stalin which caused Mandelstam's first arrest (1934). Alternative second couplet:
    "Of our voices, but each muttered half-phrase
    Sings the Kremlin mountain-man's praise."

42. What is the name of this street? ....

Ironic poem satirizing his position as a forgotten exile, banished to Voronezh, where he lived in wretched housing on the outskirts of the city.

43. The day was five-headed. For five days and
     nights ....

Impressionistic images of the Mandelstams' journey into
banishment in the Urals and of Osip's post-prison insanity.
Hearing: in Russian, same word as rumor. *Five-headed*: the
two Mandelstams, and the three guards in the escort, re-
ferred to also as "scholars of Pushkin," because Mandelstam
read Pushkin to them. *Chapayev*: early Soviet sound film,
about a Civil War cavalry hero in the Urals.

44. Wave to wave the comber runs, breaking the backs
     of waves ....

Soldier metaphor, applied to the breaking waves, in par-
ticular the Janissaries, élite troops of the Turkish Emperors.
Last line: concealed quotation from Pushkin.

45. With them and not with you or me ....

Mandelstam rhapsodizes over the suppleness of Russian
inflected word endings, and invites the reader to feel them
as living beings.

46. Where is that bound and fettered groan? ....

Counterpoint to references in lost portions of the *Ode to
Stalin*, on the latter's birthplace in the Caucasus, where
Prometheus was bound to a crag and daily had his liver torn
out by an eagle's talons. *He* (line 9): possibly Stalin.

47. Let this air be called as a witness (Verses on the
     Unknown Soldier)....................................

A long pacifist poem. *Mikhail Lermontov*: Russian poet
(1814-41), army officer slain in a duel. *Mole*: here, a unit of

measurement. *Battle of the Nations*: like the other battles named, an engagement fought by Napoleon I. *Schweik*: the stubbiness of his nose is a feature in Joseph Lada's illustrations to Czech author Jaroslav Hasek's anti-militarist comic novel. The reference to Quixote's birdlike features similarly, are taken from Daumier's paintings. The final section of the poem refers to Mandelstam's own date of birth.

48. The breaches of round bays, the gravel and the blue. . . . .

In banishment in Voronezh, Mandelstam dreams of the Black Sea. Cf. Nos. 42-44.

49. I'll say it in draft in a whisper. . . . .

In the original, the verse has a unique rhythm. *Heaven-roofed depository*: pun on the Russian words for depository, grain storage shed, and reservoir.

50. Stooping involuntarily to the empty ground . . . .

To Natasha Shtempel', a cripple who befriended the Mandelstams in Voronezh. She safeguarded many of Mandelstam's manuscripts during the years following his second arrest (May, 1938) and death.

INDEX TO TITLES

115